PHILIPPINES

Country Explorers

Anne Schraff

Lerner Publications Company • Minneapolis

Lerner Publications Company
A division of Lerner Publishing Group, Inc.
241 First Avenue North
Minneapolis, MN 55401 U.S.A.

Website address: www.lernerbooks.com

Library of Congress Cataloging-in-Publication Data

Schraff, Anne E.
      Philippines / by Anne Schraff.
         p.   cm. — (Country explorers)
      Includes index.
      ISBN 978–1–58013–596–2 (lib. bdg. : alk. paper)
      1. Philippines—Juvenile literature. I. Title.
DS655.S472 2009
959.9—dc22   2008012676

Manufactured in the United States of America
1 2 3 4 5 6 – PA – 14 13 12 11 10 09

Table of Contents

Welcome!

We're going to the Philippines! The Philippines is an island country in the southwest Pacific Ocean. The Philippines form a chain of more than seven thousand islands. They lie just southeast of the continent of Asia. The Philippines are washed by the Philippine Sea to the east. The South China Sea splashes the western coast of the Philippines. In the southwest, the Sulu Sea is between the Philippines and Malaysia. The Celebes Sea lies to the south.

Tiny islands lie just off the coast of Palawan Island in the Philippines.

PACIFIC
OCEAN

LUZON

Lucban ●

MOUNT
PINATUBO
Quezon
City
Betis ●
Manila ★

MAYON
VOLCANO

PHILIPPINE
SEA

volcano
uplands
plains
mountains

P
H
I
L
I
P
P
I
N
E
S

MINDORO

SOUTH
CHINA
SEA

BOROCAY
ISLAND

CEBU

LEYTE

Cebu City ●

PALAWAN

SULU
SEA

MINDANAO

Davao ●

MALAYSIA

SULU ARCHIPELAGO

CELEBES
SEA

Philippines

Land

Sandy beaches ring many of the Philippines' islands. Farther inland you might find steep mountains or gentle hills. In other areas, lush tropical rain forests cover the land. Some of the islands are so tiny that no one lives on them. But others, such as Luzon, are huge. Manila is the capital of the Philippines. The city sits on the island of Luzon.

The island of Boracay is a popular tourist spot in the Philippines. This part of the island is called White Beach.

Map Whiz Quiz

Take a look at the map on page 5. Trace the outline of the Philippines onto a sheet of paper. Can you find the South China Sea? Label it with a *W* for west. How about the Philippine Sea? Mark it with an *E* for east. Look for the Pacific Ocean. Label it with an *N* for north. Use a blue crayon to color in the seas that surround the islands.

The island of Luzon has the best farmland in the Philippines. People grow rice on the steep hillsides there.

The Mayon Volcano sits on Luzon. It is an active volcano. That means it can still push out smoke and lava.

Earth Movers

The islands that make up the Philippines were once totally under water. Millions of years ago, volcanoes and earthquakes worked together to push the Philippines above the surface of the Pacific Ocean.

These days, small earthquakes shake the islands at least five times each year.

How Big?

Imagine you could squeeze all the Philippine Islands together into one big landmass. You would have a country about the size of the state of Nevada.

An earthquake in the Philippines knocked down this house.

In the Tropics

The Philippines lie in a zone called the tropics. Daytime temperatures reach 80°F (27°C) most of the year. The rainy season lasts from May through November.

This street in Manila flooded during the rainy season.

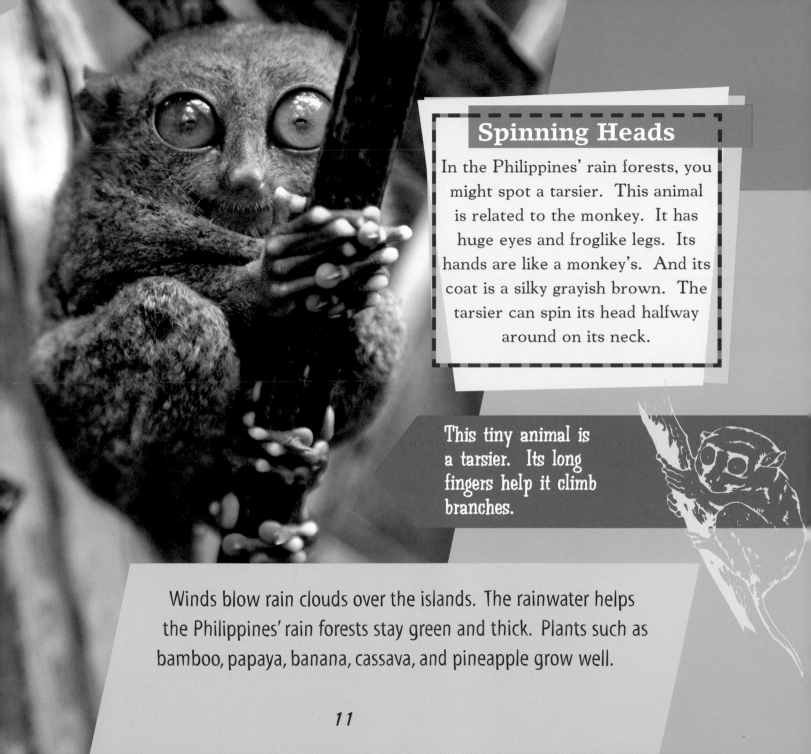

Spinning Heads

In the Philippines' rain forests, you might spot a tarsier. This animal is related to the monkey. It has huge eyes and froglike legs. Its hands are like a monkey's. And its coat is a silky grayish brown. The tarsier can spin its head halfway around on its neck.

This tiny animal is a tarsier. Its long fingers help it climb branches.

Winds blow rain clouds over the islands. The rainwater helps the Philippines' rain forests stay green and thick. Plants such as bamboo, papaya, banana, cassava, and pineapple grow well.

First Folks

As long as thirty thousand years ago, people from the Aeta ethnic group lived in the Philippines. The Aetas may have walked to the Philippines. Land may have connected the Philippines to southeastern Asia.

Aeta girls collect seashells on Boracay Island.

Many years later, the Philippines became islands. Then members of the Malay ethnic group arrived. They came from Southeast Asia in canoes. The early Malay grew rice in northern Luzon.

Following the Stars

Malay sailors watched for changes in the clouds, stars, and ocean waves. That's how they found their way to the Philippines.

People still use canoes to travel around the Philippines.

13

Filipinos

People who live in the Philippines are called Filipinos. Most Filipinos are from the Malay ethnic group. Other Filipinos belong to one of eighty other ethnic groups.

These Filipino children live in Quezon City on Luzon.

These Ifugao women wear traditional clothes. The fields behind them are full of rice plants.

The Tagalogs are a Malay people. They are the largest group in the country. Most Tagalogs live in the Manila area. Members of the Aeta, Bontoc, and Ifugao ethnic groups live in the mountains of northern Luzon. They grow rice.

Family Time

How many people are in your family? Filipino families are usually pretty big. Grandparents, parents, children, and even aunts and cousins live together. They live in a compound. A compound is a group of houses built close together. The houses are small. Most kids share bedrooms with their brothers or sisters.

This mother, daughter, and granddaughter live together in one house.

In the typical Filipino family, the father goes to work every day. He is the head of the family. Moms stay home with the kids. They also shop, cook, and pay bills.

Pakikisama

Mothers teach their children the custom of *pakikisama*. Pakikisama is a way of showing kindness and consideration to others at all times. Filipino kids learn from a young age not to yell at a store clerk for making a mistake. And they do not make fun of a schoolmate.

This mother balances a tub of clean dishes on her head.

Skyscrapers rise from the middle of Manila.

Busy Manila

In Manila, people and cars crowd the streets. Manila has lots of tall skyscrapers. The city also has brand-new shopping centers. Some city dwellers own televisions, computers, radios, and telephones. They live in new houses. They may drive speedy, new cars.

But in the city's poor areas, families live in flimsy shacks. They are made of metal and cardboard. Poor people work hard just to make enough money to buy food.

Poor people in Manila live in these tiny shacks.

Country Life

Many Filipinos live in the countryside. Most of them are rice farmers. They carve shelves of land into the hillsides and mountain slopes. The shelves are called terraces. Farmers plant rice in the wet, flat terraces. The whole family helps plant and harvest the rice. Then they sell the rice at roadside stands.

These farmers are planting rice. A field of rice is called a paddy.

Many families build their homes on stilts. The stilts keep the house out of the water during the rainy season.

This house sits close to the water. Stilts keep it from getting wet during floods.

21

Dress Up

If you are packing for the Philippines, don't forget your jeans and T-shirts. This is what most kids wear. The weather is usually warm. So people wear light clothes.

Filipino boys wear T-shirts and jeans. Some wear shorts.

In the countryside, women might wear *sayas*—long skirts. Men sometimes wear an embroidered shirt called a *barong tagalog*.

This woman wears a colorful *saya*.

Getting There

Make way for jeepneys! They are old jeeps. Filipinos have turned them into taxis. Cars, trucks, buses, and bicycles share the busy streets.

Manila Jeepney

Dear Cousin Jamal,

The Philippines is such a fun place! Yesterday I swam in the South China Sea. And I picked ripe bananas. I just took my first ride through Manila on a jeepney. Wow! A jeepney is like a taxicab. But the drivers decorate them with miniature horses, bright tassels, or anything they can think of.

See you soon.

Marcus

Y
Y
An

People get off a train that's part of the Metro Manila Light Rail Transit.

In Manila, you can catch a ride on the Metro Manila Light Rail Transit. The train runs on a track built above the streets. In the countryside, lots of people walk. Or they might ride on a water buffalo.

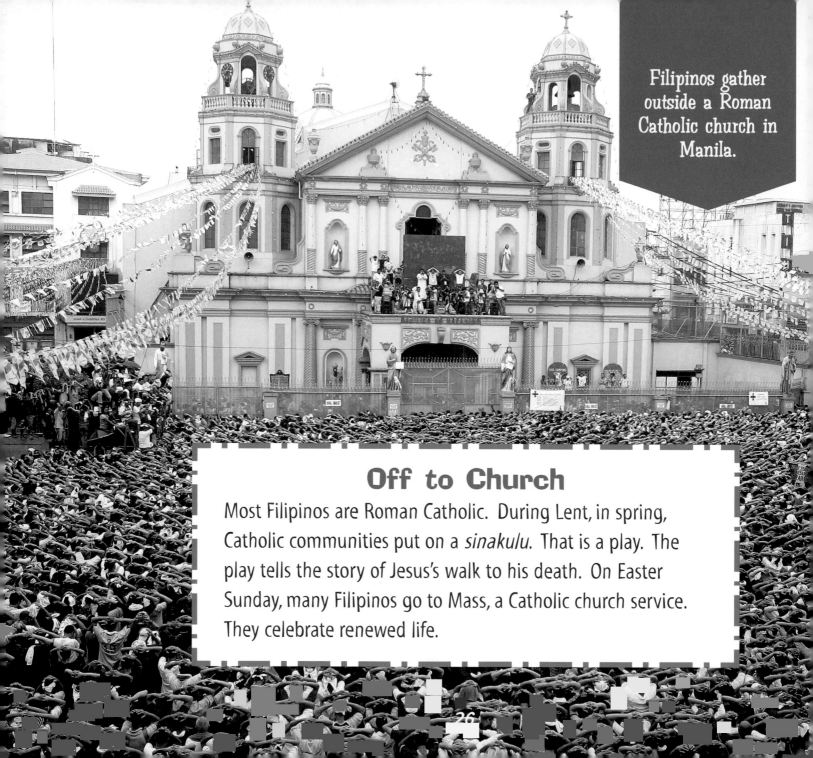

Filipinos gather outside a Roman Catholic church in Manila.

Off to Church

Most Filipinos are Roman Catholic. During Lent, in spring, Catholic communities put on a *sinakulu*. That is a play. The play tells the story of Jesus's walk to his death. On Easter Sunday, many Filipinos go to Mass, a Catholic church service. They celebrate renewed life.

Every region and city has a patron saint. Each city chooses a particular saint. The saint is honored as a special protector. Each year, towns have special holidays to honor their saints.

Hari Raya Poasa

Muslim families enjoy the Hari Raya Poasa holiday. It marks the end of a monthlong fast. During the fast, people cannot eat between sunrise and sunset. On the holiday, gongs beat on the street to start the festival. People wear their best clothes. Family members ask forgiveness of one another for past wrongs. Families have big feasts. And adults often give gifts or money to children on this special day.

People touch a statue of Saint Theresa outside a church in Manila.

Festival Time

Filipinos in the town of Lucban celebrate the feast day of San Isidro Labrador on May 15. San Isidro is the patron saint of farmers. The festival is called Pahiyas. It is a thanksgiving for a good harvest.

The day begins with Mass at San Luis Obispo Church. A parade follows. Many people dress in traditional clothing.

Dancers perform in a parade on the feast of San Isidro Labrador.

Families decorate the fronts of their houses with fruits, vegetables, grains, and flowers. They also use beautiful decorations made from dried rice paste. The rice paste is shaped into brightly colored flowers and leaves. People from all over the world come to this colorful festival.

Children peek from the window of a house on Pahiyas. The flowers and birds are made of rice paste.

Students listen to their teacher in a crowded classroom.

Small Talk

In the Philippines, people speak more than eighty different languages. Filipino is a language based on Tagalog. Filipino is one of the country's official languages. English is the other. Everyone learns Filipino in elementary school.

Half of all Filipinos speak English. They can read and write in English and Filipino.

Body Talk

Filipinos use more than just words to talk to one another. Raising the eyebrows for a moment is one way to say hello. A smile may mean someone is happy. But it may also mean that the person is trying to be friendly.

A Filipina girl works on her English lesson in a classroom.

Students work in a school garden. They have planted different kinds of vegetables.

School Days

Filipino kids study math, science, Filipino, English, history, and civics (government). They work hard to get good grades. That means doing homework. Most schools also have gardens. Kids learn how to farm in them.

Filipino families show pride in a kid's good grades. Sometimes they place a student's picture in the local paper.

A boy works hard on a test in his classroom in Manila.

Kids also take lots of tests. Teachers post grades for all the school to see. Many families throw big parties when kids earn high grades.

Rice Is Nice

Filipinos eat rice almost every day. For a great snack, Filipinos like sticky rice cakes. They also like *suman*, rice cakes wrapped in coconut or banana leaves.

A woman sells suman in a market in the Philippines.

The most popular Filipino meal is adobo. Adobo is a stew made with pork or chicken. If you are looking for something sweet, try *halo-halo*. It is a tasty dessert of fruit chunks, ice, and gelatin.

Filipinos often eat adobo with vegetables or rice.

Tell a Story

Are you in the mood to hear a good story? In the Philippines, folktales are passed down through families over many years. The stories come from Malayan, Chinese, Indian, and Muslim cultures.

Children gather at a mobile library in Manila. The van brings books and storytellers to poor neighborhoods.

"The Ape and the Firefly"

A firefly flew past a big ape one night. The ape asked the firefly why he had a little light. "To scare off mosquitoes," said the firefly. The ape laughed and said, "What a big coward you are to fear mosquitoes!"

"I'm not a coward," said the firefly. "I can beat you anytime." The ape laughed so hard he almost fell down. But then the ape stood straight and tall. He was waiting for the firefly to try to attack him. The firefly flew up and settled on the ape's nose. The ape tried to squash the firefly. The ape clamped his hand on his nose so hard that he knocked himself out. The firefly laughed. Just before the ape's hand reached his nose, the clever firefly had flown away. Ever since that day, apes have been afraid of fireflies.

Most Filipino folktales teach lessons about life. The story "The Ape and the Firefly" is one example. The story teaches that even people who may appear small and weak can use brainpower to win fights.

Art to Use

Did you ever sit on a work of art? Filipino wood-carvers make furniture from Philippine trees. Artists in the town of Betis are known for making the best furniture in the country. Betis is on the island of Luzon.

A Filipino man carves a piece of wood on the island of Luzon.

On the islands of Mindanao and Mindoro, basketmaking is the thing to do. Artists use bamboo vines. They make baskets in many different shapes, sizes, and designs.

Sweet Dreams

Mat makers weave brown sleeping mats from soft, sweet-smelling pandanus. Filipinos claim that they have the best dreams when sleeping on a fragrant mat. Eventually, the mats lose their scent. No one minds. Filipinos just buy new mats at the market.

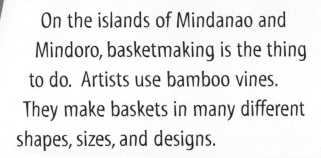

This shop sells many different types of baskets.

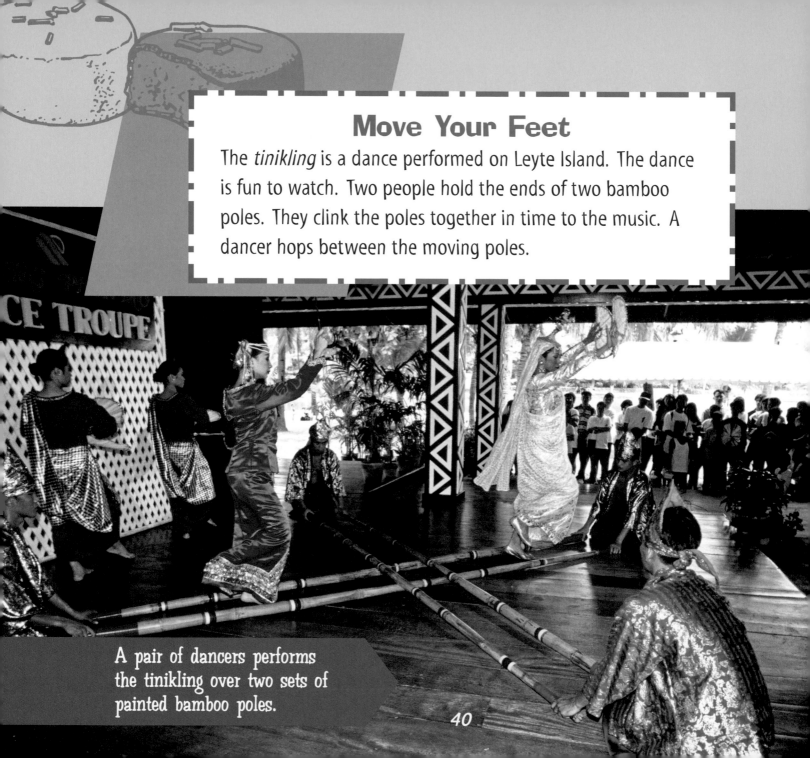

Move Your Feet

The *tinikling* is a dance performed on Leyte Island. The dance is fun to watch. Two people hold the ends of two bamboo poles. They clink the poles together in time to the music. A dancer hops between the moving poles.

A pair of dancers performs the tinikling over two sets of painted bamboo poles.

The *binusian* is another dance. Dancers balance jars that hold lit candles. The jars sit on their heads and on their outstretched hands. The music starts out slowly. But soon, the pace quickens. The dancers scramble to keep the beat and to keep the candles lit.

Filipinos love to fly all kinds of kites.

Fun Stuff

Looking for fun? Go fly a *boka-boka*. A boka-boka is a small, square kite. Kids make them out of sticks and paper.

Or try playing a game called *luksong tinik*. Two kids hold up a long stick. Another player tries to jump over it. The kids keep raising the stick. Finally, the jumpers can no longer jump over it. The kid who jumps over the stick in the highest position wins the game.

Children play in a hammock outside their home on Mindanao Island.

THE FLAG OF THE PHILIPPINES

The Philippine flag is blue, red, and white. The blue stands for noble ideals. The red represents courage. The white stands for peace. The sun on the white triangle represents independence. The stars around the sun stand for the three main groups of islands. The northern group includes Luzon and Mindoro. The central group is called the Visayan Islands. The southern group includes Mindanao and the Sulu Archipelago. The Sulu Archipelago includes about four hundred islands southwest of Mindanao.

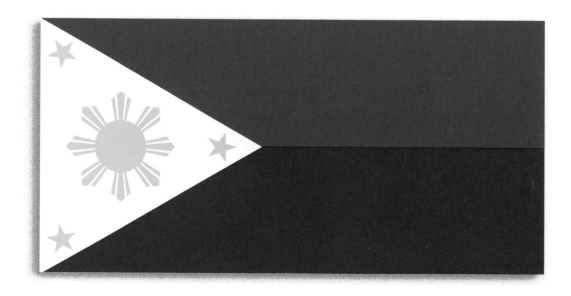

FAST FACTS

FULL COUNTRY NAME: Republic of the Philippines

AREA: 115,831 square miles (300,001 square kilometers). If you squeezed all the Philippine Islands together into one landmass, it would be about as big as the state of Nevada.

MAIN LANDFORMS: the mountain ranges Caraballo, Cordillera Central, Diuata, Katanglad, Sierra Madre, Zambales, and Zamboanga; the volcanoes Mount Apo, Mount Canlaon, Mount Mayon, Mount Pinatubo, and Mount Taal; the valleys Agusan River valley, Cagayan Valley, and Cotabato Valley; the Iloilo Plain; and the rain forests.

MAJOR RIVERS: Agusan, Cagayan, Grande, Mindanao, Pampanga, and Pasig

ANIMALS AND THEIR HABITATS: monkeys (forests), mouse deer (Palawan Island), snakes and lizards (throughout the islands), small wild buffalo called tamarau (mountains), tarsiers (rain forests), water buffalo called carabao (farms)

CAPITAL CITY: Manila

OFFICIAL LANGUAGES: English and Filipino (a form of Tagalog)

POPULATION: about 90,000,000

GLOSSARY

compound: a group of houses built close together

continent: any one of seven large areas of land. The continents are Africa, Antarctica, Asia, Australia, Europe, North America, and South America.

earthquake: the shaking of the ground caused by the shifting of underground rock

ethnic group: a group of people with many things in common, such as language, religion, and customs

folktale: a story told by word of mouth from grandparent to parent to child. Many folktales explain where an ethnic group came from or how the world began.

Lent: the forty days (except for Sundays) before Easter. Lent is a time of fasting, praying, and repenting for sins.

pandanus: a fiber made from screw pine trees. Screw pine trees have crowns of swordlike leaves.

rain forest: a thick, green forest that gets lots of rain every year

tropic zone: an area with high temperatures and plant growth year-round

volcano: an opening in Earth's surface through which hot, melted rock and gases shoot up. Volcano can also mean the hill or mountain of ash and rock that builds up around the opening.

TO LEARN MORE

BOOKS

Gray, Shirley W. *The Philippines.* New York: Scholastic, 2003.

Nickles, Greg. *The Philippines: The Civilization.* Lancaster, UK: Crabtree, 2002.

Nickles, Greg. *The Philippines: The Culture.* Lancaster, UK: Crabtree, 2002

Nickles, Greg. *Philippines: The Land.* Lancaster, UK: Crabtree, 2002.

Romolo, Liana, and Corazon Dandan-Albano. *Filipino Friends.* North Clarendon, VT: Tuttle Publishing, 2007.

Romano, Liana, and Jamie M. Laurel. *My First Book of Tagalog Words: Fililpino Rhymes and Verses.* North Clarendon, VT: Tuttle Publishing, 2007.

Tope, Lily Rose R., and Detch P. Nonan-Mercado. *Philippines.* New York: Benchmark Books, 2002.

WEBSITES

Palawan & Iligan, Philippines
http://toting.fateback.com
See plants, animals, fountains, waterfalls, and an underground river, and get a look at Philippine life.

Philippine Travel Pictures
http://www.philippinepictures.com
View a photo album of the Philippines. Get an up-close look at cities, countryside, festivals, animals, and more. Enjoy a glimpse of Philippine life.

Yahoo!.Kids Philippines—Pictures
http://kids.yahoo.com/directory/Around-the-World/Countries/Philippines/Mount-pinatubo/pictures
Visit this site to see fascinating color photos of various eruptions of Mount Pinatubo. You can also go to related sites.

INDEX